PILL BUGS & SOW BUGS
and Other Crustaceans

TEXT BY ELAINE PASCOE

PHOTOGRAPHS BY DWIGHT KUHN

BLACKBIRCH PRESS, INC.

WOODBRIDGE, CONNECTICUT

Published by Blackbirch Press, Inc.
260 Amity Road
Woodbridge, CT 06525

To Kaitlyn and Kaleb
–D.K.

Email: staff@blackbirch.com
Web site: www.blackbirch.com

Printed in the United States

10 9 8 7 6 5 4 3 2 1

front cover: pill bug
back cover: sow bug with eggs, sow bug carrying young, sow bug with molted skin, adult sow bug

Library of Congress Cataloging-in-Publication Data
Pascoe, Elaine.
Pill bugs and sow bugs and other crustaceans / by Elaine Pascoe; photographs by Dwight Kuhn
     p.   cm. — (Nature close-up)
   Includes bibliographical references (p. 47).
   ISBN 1-56711-473-3 (hardcover : alk. paper)
   1. Crustacea—Juvenile literature. 2. Crustacea—Study and teaching (Elementary)—Activity programs. [1. Wood lice (Crustaceans) 2. Crustaceans—Experiments. 3. Experiments.] I. Kuhn, Dwight, ill. II. Title.
QL437.2.P37   2001   00-011914
595.3—dc21   CIP
                                              AC

Note on metric conversions: The metric conversions given in Chapters 2 and 3 of this book are not always exact equivalents of U.S. measures. Instead, they provide a workable quantity for each experiment in metric units. The abbreviations used are:

cm	centimeter	**kg**	kilogram
m	meter	**l**	liter
g	gram	**cc**	cubic centimeter

CONTENTS

1

Crustacean Nation

Roll aside a rotting log in the woods, and tiny gray-brown creatures scurry for cover. They look like miniature armadillos. These animals are called sow bugs—but they're not really insects of any kind. These creatures belong to a different animal family, the family that includes lobsters and crabs. They are crustaceans.

The crustacean family has many members. Sow bugs and pill bugs are among the few members that live on land. Water-dwelling crustaceans are found all over the world—from polar oceans to tropical regions. They live in fresh water and seawater, in shallow ponds and ocean depths. Some crustaceans even live in hot springs!

Fossils show that the first crustaceans appeared on Earth at least 500 million years ago. Today there are about 26,000 different kinds, or species, of crustaceans. Besides lobsters, crabs, pill bugs, and sow bugs, crustaceans include shrimps, crayfish, beach fleas, barnacles, and lots of less familiar animals.

Crayfish are just one of many kinds of animals that belong to the crustacean family.

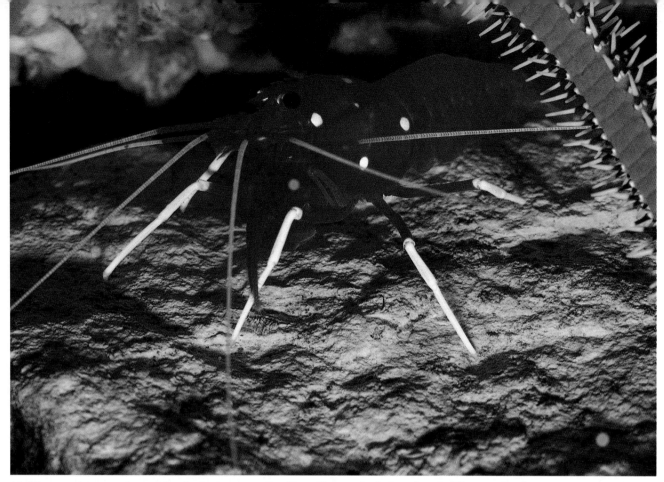
Unlike sow bugs and most land crustaceans, the Hawaiian crab shrimp is a brilliant red color.

SHELL GAME

Crustaceans differ as much in appearance as they do in size. Their colors range from the drab gray-brown of sow bugs to the brilliant red of deep-sea shrimp. Many tiny ocean crustaceans have no color at all—their bodies are transparent. Some glow like fireflies. They are bioluminescent. The smallest crustaceans can only be seen under a microscope. The biggest, the Japanese spider crab, can stretch its legs out to span 12 feet (3.6 m)!

For all their differences, crustaceans—from beach fleas to giant crabs—have a lot in common. Instead of a bony skeleton, a crustacean has an exoskeleton—a hard outer shell. This shell is made of protein and a material called chitin. Like a little suit of armor, the shell is divided into segments, so the animal can move around. The number of segments may be anywhere from 6 to 60, depending on the species.

Most crustaceans have three main body regions—head, thorax, and abdomen. The head holds the animal's brain, sensory organs, and mouth. The thorax holds the heart, stomach, and reproductive organs. The abdomen holds the intestines.

Right: The outer shell of a crustacean is divided into segments for ease of movement.
Below: The head and eyes of a sow bug.

Crustaceans have two pairs of antennae, which sense their surroundings by touch, smell, and taste. The shape, size, and structure of crustacean eyes vary greatly. The smallest crustaceans have simple eyes that probably can't do much more than detect light. Many other crustaceans have compound eyes, like the eyes of insects. On some of these animals—including lobsters and crabs—the eyes are on stalks. That makes it easy for the animal to look around. Cave shrimp, which live in underground pools, are eyeless. In their dark world, they don't need to see.

Left: **The eyes of some crustaceans, like this hermit crab, are located on stalks.**
Below: **Many crustaceans are able to see quite well.**

Jointed legs are a common crustacean feature.

Jointed legs are another feature of crustaceans, but the number and design of their legs differ with the species. Some are designed for walking, some for swimming, and some for gathering food. Some crustaceans even have legs specially adapted for carrying their eggs and young.

Crustaceans don't have lungs. The smallest crustaceans take in oxygen through their body surfaces. Most crustaceans breathe through gills, just like fish do. Gills are often located on the animal's legs or sides. As water flows through a crustacean's gills, oxygen from the water is drawn into its body. Even crustaceans that live on land—sow bugs, pill bugs, and land crabs—have gills. It's very important for their gills to stay moist, so these animals are usually found in damp places.

FAMILY MEMBERS

Scientists group crustaceans into more than 30 orders, based on body features and other physical traits. Sow bugs and their close relatives, pill bugs, look very much alike. Both of these crustaceans are also called wood lice. Wood lice feed mainly on dead plants and other decaying matter. They have seven pairs of legs and oval bodies that measure less than half an inch long. How can you tell a sow bug from a pill bug? When a pill bug is disturbed, it rolls into a tight little ball. Because of this response, "roly-poly" is another name for this animal. Sow bugs can't roll up. A sow bug also has a pair of sharp stalks on its tail end.

Left top and bottom, and opposite: **When a pill bug becomes frightened, it will curl itself into a ball and remain like that until danger passes.**

There are thousands of different kinds of sow bugs and pill bugs worldwide. These animals first came to North America from Europe—probably in the boats that carried European settlers. They are members of the isopod crustacean order. "Isopod" means "equal legged." These crustaceans have legs that are all the same length.

Brine shrimp, water fleas, and about 900 other kinds of little crustaceans belong to the branchiopod order. As they swim, branchiopods beat the water with their feathery legs, trapping algae and other tiny bits of food. Water fleas live in fresh water worldwide. Brine shrimp, sometimes called sea monkeys, are found in briny ponds that often have a higher salt content than the oceans. Most brine shrimp are only about half an inch long, but they are true survivors. If the water in their pond evaporates, they form protective cysts around themselves and become inactive. They spring back to life when the water returns.

Top: **Brine shrimp are found in very salty water.** *Bottom:* **Water fleas only live in fresh water.**

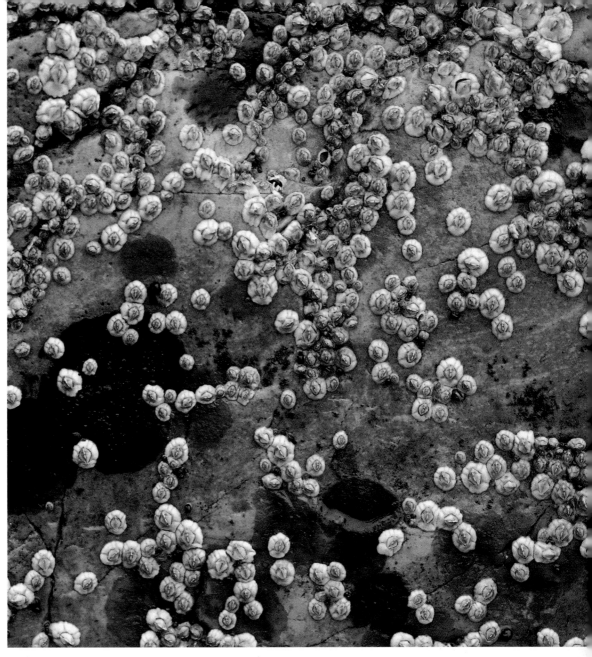

As barnacles get older, they permanently attach themselves to hard surfaces.

Barnacles also filter water for food. These odd little crustaceans begin life swimming freely in the ocean. But as they get older, they attach themselves head first to rocks, pilings, and boat hulls. A barnacle then grows a thick shell and spends the rest of its life in that spot. To eat, it sticks its legs out of its shell and fans a stream of water toward its mouth, collecting microscopic bits of food.

Sometimes barnacles are left "high and dry" when the tide goes out. The lack of water, however, hardly affects these little crustaceans. They simply close their shells and wait for the water to come back. Barnacles are odd in another way. In most crustaceans the two sexes are separate. But many barnacles are both male and female— that is, each one has both male and female reproductive organs.

A barnacle stretches its legs out of its shell to collect food.

Many crabs have powerful claws on their front legs.

Crabs, lobsters, crayfish, and true shrimps belong to the decapod crustacean group. "Decapod" means "ten legged." In true lobsters and many crabs, the front legs end in powerful claws. These animals use their claws for defense and to catch and crush food—mainly fish, shellfish, and other crustaceans. Lobsters, crayfish, and crabs can actually re-grow legs that are lost in battles with predators. This process is called regeneration.

Beach fleas and scuds are members of a different crustacean group. These small creatures are scavengers—they eat dead animals and plant material. Scuds, which look like tiny shrimp, eat debris that floats in the water. Beach fleas, which look like sow bugs, eat dead fish and other material that wash up on the shore.

Scuds eat floating debris in the water.

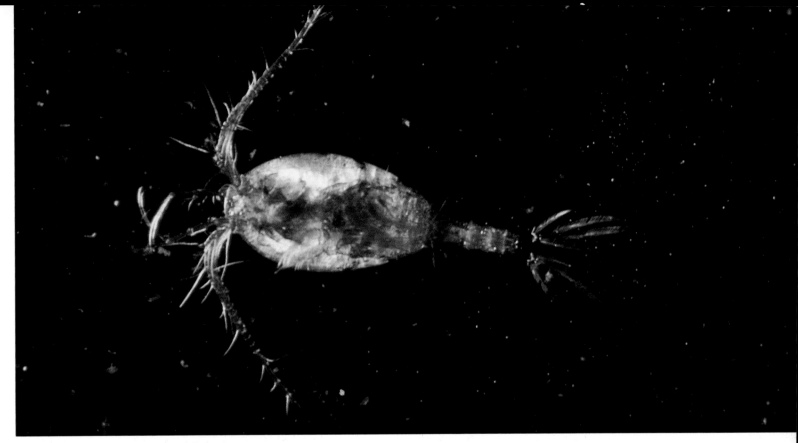

Copepods are some of the smallest crustaceans.

Copepods include some of the smallest crustaceans—less than 8/1,000 inch (0.2 mm) in length. Some copepods feed on seaweed after they burrow into the plants. Others are parasites that live on different ocean creatures. One type of copepod lives in the mouths of certain large whales. It feeds on algae that grow on the whale's baleen. The baleen is a sort of strainer that the whale uses to filter food from the water.

Free-swimming copepods are part of plankton—a microscopic mix of plant and animal matter that floats in the ocean. Plankton is a key link in the ocean food chain. Many larger ocean animals depend on plankton to survive.

EGG TO ADULT

Most crustaceans come into the world in more or less the same way. Males and females mate, and the females lay eggs. Some time later, the eggs hatch.

Wood lice mate in spring. A female may carry up to 200 eggs in a pouch on the underside of her body. The eggs hatch 3 to 7 weeks after mating, and the young remain in the pouch for about 6 weeks after that. Then the young are ready to go off on their own.

A female sow bug can carry young on the underside of her body.

Freshwater crayfish (sometimes called crawfish or crawdads) mate in fall. The female carries thousands of eggs, along with sperm from the male, throughout winter. In spring, she releases the eggs, and they combine with the sperm. The crayfish glues the eggs to her small hind legs (called swimmerets) with a sticky substance. She curls her tail over the eggs to protect them until they are ready to hatch, in 5 to 8 weeks. The young crayfish stay with their mother for a time before swimming off on their own.

Above: Crayfish look for mates in the fall.
Below: A female sow bug can keep up to 200 eggs in a pouch under her body.

Many newly hatched crustaceans, or larvae, don't look much like their parents. Lobster larvae look like little shrimps, for example. But as they grow, their bodies change. Most crustaceans go through several distinct stages on the way to adulthood.

Young crayfish huddle in a pouch under their mother's tail.

STRENGTH IN NUMBERS

Krill, small shrimp-like crustaceans that thrive in cold ocean waters, are the most abundant animals on Earth—at least in terms of total body mass. A single krill is only about 2 inches (5 cm) long, but millions often swarm together in the oceans. Penguins, seals, whales, and many other animals eat krill. In fact, a blue whale can swallow 4 tons of krill a day!

Krill are especially important in the Antarctic, where they are at the base of the food chain. Krill gather under the ice sheets that cover Antarctic seas. Their larvae mature there, hiding in cracks and caves in the ice. In recent years, a worldwide warming trend has caused some of the sea ice to melt. That has scientists worried. Less ice means fewer krill—and that could mean trouble for the many animals that depend on these tiny crustaceans for food.

American lobsters molt several times each year.

As young crustaceans get bigger, they outgrow their hard exoskeletons. Then the crustaceans must molt, or shed the old shell. When the shell splits, the animal wiggles out. Its new shell is soft, and the animal swells up with water to stretch it out to a roomier size. Until the new shell hardens, the crustacean is at great risk from predators.

Some crustaceans stop molting once they reach adult size. Others keep growing and molting. Adult American lobsters molt several times a year and slowly grow throughout their lives. Most weigh 2 to 3 pounds (0.9 to 1.4 kg), but some become giants. The largest lobster ever found weighed more than 44 pounds (20 kg)!

This sow bug is sitting next to its molted skin.

CRUSTACEANS AND PEOPLE

Most people have probably seen more crustaceans on the dinner table than anywhere else. Shrimps, crabs, lobsters, and crayfish are eaten in many parts of the world. These large crustaceans are netted and trapped in great numbers. Over-fishing has caused the numbers of some types to shrink, especially true lobsters.

In some cases, people have taken too many crustaceans from their natural habitats.

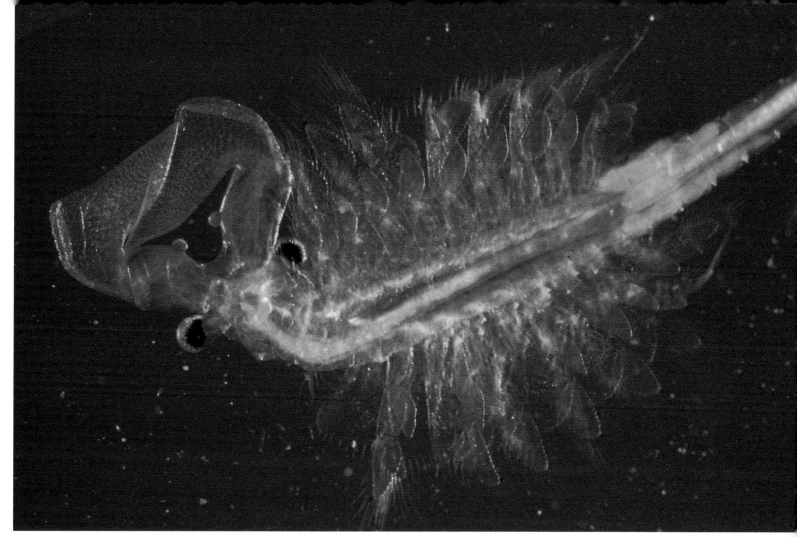

Brine shrimp are often used as fish food.

Small crustaceans may be on your dinner table, too—although you may not be aware of it. These tiny creatures are netted in vast numbers. They may be used in seafood pastes that are ingredients in processed foods. A type of brine shrimp that lives in Great Salt Lake, Utah, is widely used as food for fish in aquariums.

LOOKING FOR A HOME

Hermit crabs are different from all other crabs in an important way. While most other crabs are completely protected by their own hard shells, a hermit crab's abdomen is soft. To protect itself from predators, it "borrows" an empty snail shell and pushes its abdomen inside the shell. The crab then carries the shell along as it searches for food. If danger threatens, the crab pulls its entire body into the shell. Eventually, it outgrows its borrowed shell and must search for a larger one.

Left: A hermit crab without its shell. *Right:* A hermit crab must look for a new shell as its body grows.

Sometimes crustaceans can be pests. Barnacles that attach themselves to a ship's hull can slow the ship down, forcing it to use more fuel. Gribbles—small relatives of sow bugs—attack the wood pilings of piers. Gribbles dig shallow tunnels in the wood, which causes serious damage.

Most crustaceans, however, are harmless or even helpful. Pill bugs, sow bugs, beach fleas, and many others are members of the natural "clean-up squad" that breaks down and recycles dead plant and animal matter. These odd little animals, in their suits of armor, are also very interesting to watch.

Beach fleas break down, and feed on, dead plant and animal matter.

2

Caring for Wood Lice and Brine Shrimp

Crustaceans are easy to spot if you live near the ocean. You can find barnacles, crabs, beach fleas, and other species along the water's edge. These animals shouldn't be taken from the wild, however, because it's difficult to provide them with the conditions they need to survive.

Away from the coast, members of this animal family may be harder to find. Wood lice are the big exception—sow bugs and pill bugs are just about everywhere. And, unlike many other crustaceans, they are easy to keep and care for. That makes them good subjects for observation.

This chapter explains how to collect and care for pill bugs and sow bugs. You'll also find out how to buy and hatch brine shrimp.

Although most crustaceans live along the sea coast, some can also be found in freshwater ponds and marshes.

COLLECTING WOOD LICE

Pill bugs and sow bugs are active at night. During the day, they hide in damp places—underneath stones, bricks, wood planks, logs, fallen branches, and leaf piles. You may find them hiding in a shady part of your yard, or even in a damp corner of your basement. Sometimes you may need to take a walk in the woods to find them, but take along an adult if you do.

Remember that other kinds of animals may also make their homes in the same places where wood lice live. Some, such as snakes and wasps, are animals that you won't want to disturb! Use a long stick to roll aside a rotting log or move leaf piles, so you can see exactly what's underneath without getting too close.

Some wood lice make their homes under stones and in wood piles.

Bring a small glass container for collecting the wood lice. Punch small holes in the lid, so that air can get in. It's very important for wood lice to stay moist at all times—they will die if they dry out. To prevent that, put some damp sand or moist (but not soggy) soil in the container. Add a flat stone or a piece of damp wood that the animals can hide under.

Collect just a few of the wood lice you find. Carefully use tweezers to put them into your container, or gently prod them in with a small stick. Then return the log, stone, or whatever else you moved to its original position, so that the other animals that live under it will stay damp.

Use tweezers to carefully place wood lice into a collection jar.

A temporary home for wood lice should be moist and cool, and should allow air to enter.

A HOME FOR WOOD LICE

You can keep your wood lice in your collection container, or you can make a bigger home for them. A shallow plastic container works best. It should have a top that lets air in without letting too much moisture out. Try using plastic wrap with air vents (the kind sold for storing vegetables) secured with a rubber band. Or use a plastic lid with many small holes punched in it.

Fresh food that is moist works best for wood lice.

Put a layer of damp sand or moist soil on the bottom. Also give the animals something to hide under, such as a stone or a piece of damp wood. Wood lice will hide most of the time, so you will have to lift this shelter to see them. Keep the container in a cool, shady place. If the sand or soil begins to dry out, mist it lightly with a little water. Be careful not to add so much water that the layer becomes soupy.

For food, give the wood lice small pieces of ripe fruit and vegetables, such as apples, potatoes, and bits of lettuce. Tuck the food along the edges of their hiding place, so they can find it easily. Replace the food every day or so, because they will not eat it when it begins to dry out.

When you have finished watching your wood lice, take them back to the place where you found them, and let them go.

RAISING BRINE SHRIMP

If you raise brine shrimp at home, you can watch the tiny larvae swimming around, upside down, beating their tiny swimming legs up to 200 times a minute. The brine shrimp will be very small at first, but they will soon grow to their full size—about a half-inch long.

You can buy dried brine shrimp eggs at most aquarium stores or biological supply companies. Some mail-order sources are listed on page 46. You can also buy kits that contain everything you need to raise and feed the brine shrimp. Or you can make your own brine solution and food for the shrimp, as described on page 35.

Top: **Brine shrimp eggs are very small.**
Bottom: **An adult brine shrimp grows to about half an inch long.**

What to Do:

1. Make a brine solution by mixing non-iodized salt and spring water or aged water (water that has been allowed to stand, uncovered, for 24 hours). For each quart of water, add one tablespoon of salt. Pour the solution into your bowl.

2. Sprinkle a pinch of brine shrimp eggs (20 to 50 eggs) on the surface the water. Keep the bowl at room temperature, in bright light but not direct sunlight. The eggs should hatch in about 2 days.

3. To feed the larvae, mix a small amount of dry yeast (about 1/8 teaspoon) with 1 or 2 ounces of spring water or aged water. Add a small amount of this solution to the shrimp container—just enough to make the water slightly cloudy. When the water clears, in a day or so, add a bit more. If you have a fish tank with algae growing in it, put a small amount of algae in the shrimp container, too.

4. Mark the side of the brine shrimp container to show the original water level. When the level falls, add a little spring water or aged water to bring it back to the mark.

Use a little of the yeast-water solution to feed brine shrimp.

Investigating Wood Lice and Brine Shrimp

Wood lice and brine shrimp are easy to find and care for. They're also interesting to watch. In the pages that follow, you'll find some experiments and activities that will help you learn more about these little crustaceans. Have fun with these activities. When you are done, remember to return wood lice you collected in the wild to the place where you found them. Brine shrimp hatched from store-bought eggs should not be released, as they'll be unlikely to survive.

DO WOOD LICE PREFER LIGHT OR DARKNESS?

Are pill bugs and sow bugs attracted to light, or do they seek out darkness? Based on what you've read about wood lice, decide what you think. Then do this experiment. Sow bugs are shown here, but pill bugs work just as well.

What to Do:

1. Set up your container in bright light, but not direct sunlight.
2. Cover half the container with a dark towel or dark paper. Be sure to cover the sides as well as the top on that half.
3. Place several wood lice in the center of the container.

Results: Which way did the wood lice go—to the dark or light side?

Conclusions: What do the results tell you about the conditions that wood lice prefer? Can you think of reasons why the wood lice behaved as they did?

What You Need:
* Shallow, flat-bottomed container, with a moist paper towel on the bottom
* Dark towel or dark paper
* Several sow bugs or pill bugs

What You Need:

* Shallow container, with a moist paper towel on the bottom
* Tweezers
* Watch or clock with a second hand
* Pill bug

DO PILL BUGS UNROLL FASTER IN SUNLIGHT OR SHADE?

Pill bugs roll up into tight little balls when they're disturbed. When they sense that the coast is clear, they unroll and walk away. Will they unroll sooner in bright sunlight or in shade? Decide what you think. Do this experiment to see if you are right.

What to Do

1. Set up your shallow container in a sunny place.
2. Gently pick up a pill bug with tweezers. This will make it roll into a ball.
3. Place the pill bug in the container, and note how long it takes the animal to unroll and start walking.
4. Repeat the steps with the container in a shady spot.

Results: Did the pill bug unroll and walk around in the same amount of time in both locations, or did it move more quickly in one?
Conclusions: What do your results tell you about the effect of strong light on pill bugs?

WHERE DO WOOD LICE LIKE TO HIDE?

If you're hunting for wood lice, you may search under rocks, damp wood, dry wood, and leaves. Which of these places do you think wood lice like best? Make your best guess, and then do this experiment with sow bugs or pill bugs to find out.

What to Do:

1. Set up the container in a cool, shady place. Arrange the leaf, rock, and wood pieces in it.
2. Put the wood lice in the center of the container.
3. Watch to see which way the wood lice go. Leave them in the container for a while, and then check under the different materials to see where they are.

Results: Which hiding spot had the most wood lice? Try the experiment again, with the materials in different places. Are the results the same?

Conclusions: Based on this experiment, where would you be most likely to find wood lice?

What You Need:
* Shallow, flat-bottomed container, with a moist paper towel on the bottom
* Equal-sized pieces of:
  - Dry wood
  - Damp, rotting wood
  - Dry leaf
  - Flat rock
* Several wood lice

39

ARE BRINE SHRIMP ATTRACTED TO LIGHT?

Brine shrimp never seem to stop swimming. Is there a purpose to their paddling? This experiment will help you find out if they swim toward or away from light. Before you begin, decide which way you think they'll go, based on what you know.

What You Need:

* Tall, clear-sided container
* Brine solution (see page 35)
* Brine shrimp
* Flashlight

What to Do:

1. Fill the container with brine solution, as described on page 35, and add brine shrimp. (You can pour them, gently, from another container.) Put the container in a dimly lit room.
2. Aim the flashlight at the top of the container. Watch to see where the brine shrimp go.
3. Now aim the light at the bottom of the container, and watch again.

Results: Did the brine shrimp move toward or away from the light?

Conclusions: What do your results tell you about the effect of light on brine shrimp? If you did the first experiment in this chapter, compare those results to these. Did wood lice and brine shrimp react in the same way?

Note: This experiment can also be done with a shallow, flat container. Shine the light first on one side of the container, and then on the other.

To investigate how brine shrimp react to light, first shine the flashlight on the top of the jar.
Then move the light to the bottom of the container.

What You Need:

* 2 containers, both the same size (baby-food jars work well)
* Brine solution (see page 35)
* Brine shrimp eggs

DO BRINE SHRIMP EGGS HATCH FASTER IN WARM WATER OR COLD WATER?

All living things need the right conditions to grow and thrive. How does water temperature affect brine shrimp eggs? Decide if you think warmth will help them hatch or not. Then do this experiment to find out.

What to Do:

1. Put an equal amount of brine solution in each container. The amount of salt dissolved in each solution should be the same.
2. Add the same amount of brine shrimp eggs to each container. Use a small amount, such as 1/8 teaspoon.
3. Put the containers in places where the temperature will be different, but where light and other conditions will be the same. For example, put one in the refrigerator or basement (cool and dark). Put the other in a cupboard or closet in your house (warm and dark).
4. Check often to see if the eggs have hatched. The tiny larvae may be hard to see at first. Try shining a flashlight on the water—you may see them moving in the beam of light.

Results: Did the eggs hatch at the same time, or did those in one container hatch first?

Conclusions: What do the results tell you about the conditions brine shrimp need to thrive?

Above: Add 1/8 teaspoon of eggs to each jar.
Right: A light may help you see the newly
hatched brine shrimp.

43

MORE ACTIVITIES WITH CRUSTACEANS

1. Use a magnifying glass to study a wood louse. How many antennae does it have? How many segments? Can you locate its eyes?

2. Watch a wood louse walk. If you block the animal's path with an obstacle, what does it do? If you turn a wood louse onto its back, can it put itself right side up?

3. If you live near the ocean, look for crustaceans such as crabs and beach fleas at the shore. Watch these animals to see how they live in the wild. If you live near fresh water ponds and streams where crayfish live, you may be able to observe them. Take an adult along whenever you visit the water.

Top: A magnifying glass shows the details of a wood louse.
Bottom: How many crayfish can you find camouflaged among the rocks?

44

RESULTS AND CONCLUSIONS

Here are some possible results and conclusions for the activities on pages 37 to 43. Many factors may affect the results of these activities. If your results differ, try to think of reasons why. Repeat the activity with different conditions, and see if your results change.

Do wood lice prefer light or darkness?

Pill bugs and sow bugs prefer darkness. They're more likely to dry out in strong light, so they avoid it.

Do pill bugs unroll faster in sunlight or shade?

Pill bugs are usually quick to move out of strong sunlight. They seem to be in a hurry to get out of the light.

Where do wood lice like to hide?

At first, the wood lice may run for cover under the closest object. But over time, they're likely to prefer damp wood to the other materials. Moisture is very important for these animals.

Are brine shrimp attracted to light?

Unlike wood lice, brine shrimp are drawn to light. Some people raise brine shrimp as food for other animals, and they often use lights to collect them.

Do brine shrimp eggs hatch faster in warm water or cold water?

Brine shrimp eggs seem to do best in water that's room temperature or slightly warmer.

Fiddler crabs are common sights at the shore.

SOME WORDS ABOUT CRUSTACEANS

Bioluminescent Able to produce light.

Compound eyes Eyes that have many facets, or lenses.

Exoskeleton The hard outer skin or shell of a crustacean. It takes the place of an internal skeleton.

Fossils Preserved traces of ancient life.

Gills Organs that allow animals such as fish and crustaceans to draw oxygen from water.

Larvae The early forms of animals that change as they become adults.

Molt To shed the outer skin.

Scavengers Animals that eat dead plant and animal material.

Segments Sections.

Swimmerets Small hind legs used in swimming.

SOURCES FOR BRINE SHRIMP

Many aquarium and pet stores sell brine shrimp eggs as fish food. You can also buy them through the mail. Brine shrimp are sometimes sold as "sea monkeys." Two mail-order sources are:

Carolina Biological Supply
2700 York Road
Burlington, NC 27215
(800) 334-5551

Connecticut Valley Biological
82 Valley Road, P.O. Box 326
Southampton, MA 01073
(800) 628-7748

FOR MORE INFORMATION

Books

Bredeson, Carmen. *Tide Pools*. Danbury, CT: Franklin Watts, 1999.

Cerullo, Mary M. *Lobsters: Gangsters of the Sea*. New York, NY: Cobblehill, 1994.

Ricciuti, Edward R. *Crustaceans*. Woodbridge, CT: Blackbirch Press, 1994.

Ross, Michael Elsohn. *Rolypolyology*. Minneapolis, MN: Carolrhoda, 1995.

Schaffer, Donna. *Pillbugs*. Mankato, MN: Capstone Press, 1999.

Shahan, Sherry. *Barnacles Eat With Their Feet*. Brookfield, CT: Millbrook Press, 1996.

Stefoff, Rebecca. *Crab*. Tarrytown, NY: Benchmark Books, 1998.

Web Site

Lobsters (Gulf of Maine Aquarium)
Everything you could ever want to know about lobsters, including how to hypnotize one—**http://octopus.gma.org/lobsters**

INDEX

Note: Page numbers in italics indicate pictures.